A Tide Of Voices

and

Whisperings In The Grass

TWO FULL LENGTH PLAYS

By Suzanne Granfield

SAMUEL FRENCH, INC.

25 WEST 45TH STREET NEW YORK 10036

7623 SUNSET BOULEVARD HOLLYWOOD 90046

LONDON *TORONTO*

Printed in U.S.A.

ISBN 0 573 60042 2

A TIDE OF VOICES

''Insistently through sleep—
A tide of voices—
They meet you listening
In your dreams''

Hart Crane

CAST

1 woman

4 men

female singer-guitarist

No Scenery

A Tide Of Voices

(SINGER—*hum on open sound* $\overline{oo}$ *Chorus of* Johnny Has Gone For A Soldier, *establish, and continue under* VOICES.)

VOICES. (*Alternate.*)
John Gibson
Benjamin Dole
Asa Pollard
Mathew Cummings
Jason Russell
John Russell
John Eaton
Thomas Calbourn
Issac Hobart
Samuel Nelson
Asa Cram
Asahel Nins
Simeon Pike
John Alexander
Peter Fisk
William Warrin
Ceasar Bason
Daniel McGrath
Chambers Corey
John Laurence
Phineas Nevens
Thomas Wheat
Caleb Dalton

NARRATOR. (*Over names and singer* [V. O.].)
Names,
Eroded on monuments,
Dusty on plaques,
Weather streaked on corner stones.
These are not the aristocratic,
The erudite,
The thrilling.
These are simple men;
Fathers, sons, sweethearts,
Husbands, lovers, brothers,
Who gave to the cause of freedom
Not lofty retoric, or inspiring song,
Not witty phrase, or sardonic rhyme
But
The gift of life . . .
Their lives

(SINGER—*out.*)

(*Sound—Wind, establish, and continue under* VOICES *and* NARRATOR.)

Isaac Adams
Jonas Parker
Issac Mussey
Samuel Hadley
John Brown
Ashabel Porter
Jonathan Harrington

NARRATOR. (*Over names and wind.*)
It is April 19 in Lexington Massachusetts, in the year of our Lord . . . 1775

(*Wind—up, then fade as* RUTH HARRINGTON *begins to speak.*)

RUTH HARRINGTON. I shall never forget that morning. Jonathan and I had slept with the window open for spring had come early to Lexington that year. In the grey mist of dawn I could see the new buds on the walnut tree that Uncle Moses Harrington had planted between our front door and the comon. I'm not sure what wakened me . . . It was a sound—almost like faint distant thunder . . . but never stopping. Then I heard— (*Sound—Tolling Meeting House Bell.*) the dread tolling of the meeting house bell . . . the excited voices on and on . . . (*Sound—Distant Firing of Musket 3 Times.*) the signal gun!

PAUL REVERE. The Regulars Are Coming! The Regulars Are Coming!

MINUTE MAN. Get Your Musket, Jonathan Harrington!

PAUL REVERE. The Regulars Are Coming!

RUTH HARRINGTON. And come they did—800 of them, appearing like scarlet ghosts out of the grey mist. Ahead of them, like the devil himself, in his blood-red coat, astride a black horse, Major John Pitcairn, swinging his sword and shouting:

PITCAIRN. Lay down your arms, you damned rebels, or you are all dead men!

RUTH HARRINGTON. Dear God, there were only 65 of our

men: young Cousin Cleb, and Grandfather Harrington, Old Jediah Monroe with his sword . . . 12 boys in their early teens . . . Not all of them had guns! The Redcoats kept coming! Uncle John Parker cried out:

PARKER. Don't fire unless fired upon. But if they want a war, let it Begin Here!

RUTH HARRINGTON. Some of the boys began to run, but not old Jonas Parker or Ashabel Porter—or my Jonathan. Someone—as God is my witness, I couldn't tell who—cried:

MINUTE MAN. Fire! By God, Fire!

RUTH HARRINGTON. I heard a single shot . . .

(*Sound—Gun, reverberate*.)

SINGER. (*Guitar accompaniment, tune—original*.)
By the rude bridge that arched the flood,
Their flag to April's breeze unfurled,
Here on, the embattled farmers stood
And fired the shot, heard—round the world*

RUTH HARRINGTON. Oh God in heaven, it was all over so fast . . . shot after shot rang out . . . Men screamed! . . . I couldn't see my Jonathan . . . I ran for the front door, young Johnny holding onto my skirts. "Please, please go back!" Men were shouting, running past our house. I couldn't make out anything for the gun smoke:

MINUTE MAN. They got 8 of our boys!

RUTH HARRINGTON. Jonathan! Dear God, please not Jonathan! I held little Johnny's hand hard and strained to see.

(*Guitar—under——tune* What A Court Hath Old England, *slow tempo*.)

* Ralph Waldo Emerson

RUTH HARRINGTON. Just what I saw, I don't know . . . They tell me that Jonathan had been struck down near the walnut tree . . . and that he must have crawled . . . 100 yards . . . to die on his own doorstep . . . All I remember . . . is Johnny crying . . . and my kneeling down, on my doorstep . . . by my Jonathan . . . down . . . down . . . down

(SINGER—*Soft hum verse* Yankee Doodle, *slow tempo*.)

MAN. (*Softly over hum.*) Is life so dear or peace so sweet as to be purchased at the price of chains and slavery? Forbid it almighty God. I know not what course others may take; but as for me, give me liberty or give me death.*

SINGER. (*Acappella, slow tempo. Tune* Yankee Doodle, *chorus; verse, chorus—Lyrics—*Granfield.)

Stand up Jonathan,
Stand beside thy neighbor.
Grandsire, lead with your treasured sword,
We'll cross the fields together.
. . . . (*Begin Guitar accompaniment.*
. . . . *Accelerate to true tempo.*)
Our men did line the Concord Road
Behind the rocks and bushes:
With home-made guns shot sharp and straight
Without too many misses.

Heigh ho for Lexington.
Heigh ho Nantasket.
We'll send the Lobster-backs to home
A'squirmin' in a basket.
. . . .
. . . .

* Patrick Henry

In the seven towns they heard the call,
A'ringin' through the foot-hills
They left their farms; they left their shops
For musterin' and gun drills.

Yankee Doodle, Doodle doo,
Yankee Doodle Dandy
Take shovels and your pitch-forks too,
You'll find they come in handy.

(*Guitar continues one chorus under* ELI VAN MEER.)

ELI VAN MEER. Hans Pheiffer called me to muster. He said, "Eli Van Meer, it is time to go. We must pull foot for liberty." Old Hans was 78. We cleared farms for ourselves side by each. Tracked the fox by his black foot-prints in the snow. Old Hans could pop the eyes out of a bob-cat across a corn field . . . but that was two score back. Now he knows the yellowness of corn only by the juice on his fingers. Hans and I, we cleared this land . . . he with his six sons, me with three. Forced it to yield. Good crops. Broke the stones. Sowed our seed. Buried our dead . . . his Johanna, my Hilda . . . Peter, Jan . . . some without names . . . back into this land, our land. Hans said now all the young men had pulled foot for liberty, it is time for us to go. We would be the old mens company—not a man under 40. Said that we old timers must now fight to preserve our liberty. We had more years to savor the taste of it than the young men. I didn't speak sharp up. My thoughts come slow now, slow as my legs. I chewed on it a spell . . . at harvesting my shrunken belly would often ache in this new land . . . but the taste of freedom is sweet to a man . . . "Yes," I said. "Yes, I want to go." It was right and fitting. I shall take my gun . . . and my horse, for I can see best . . . furtherest off . . .

(*Guitar—drum rolls, 5th string over 6th string at 7th fret—* Death March—*under* VOICES.)

VOICES. (*Alternate.*)
Eli Van Meer
Hans Pheiffer
Jan Hals
Issac Whitcomb
Amos Wheeler
Nathaniel Parker
Ebenezer Laughton
Jonathan Hadley
Abraham Blood
Benjamin Easty
Joshua Haynes

PETER BOWEN. (*Override after* "Abram Blood.") I was still tryin' to dig in—Great Jehovah, I was thirsty—I'd nothin' to eat nor drink since we left Boston at sundown yesterd'y. Oh, Lord Almighty, it wasn't even sun-up when the first round-shot came skitterin' in! It hit Asa Pollard. Tore his leg right off! It flopped down next to him—all smashed and bloody. There's some of his blood right here on my jerkin. I can tell you I wanted to run. Bunker Hill's just over the river from Boston. I could have made it back to Hollis Hall in ten minutes. But I kept on diggin'. I wasn't goin' to have Isreal Putnam swing a sword at me like he did to Seth Cobb!

ISREAL PUTNAM. Get back to that diggin' or I'll run you through on the spot. Do you believe me now! If anyone else is thinkin' of leavin' he'll get more than just the tip of this sword!

PETER BOWEN. Lordy, that old Putnam, he killed a wolf with his bare hands down in Connecticut.

ISREAL PUTNAM. Don't fire until you see the whites of their eyes, then fire low. Take aim at their waistbands. You're all marksmen, men, and there's not one of you that can't kill a squirrel at 100 yards. Reserve your fire and we will destroy everyone of them. Aim at them handsome coats! Pick off the commanders!

PETER BOWEN. Yes sir, Capt. Putnam! . . . Lord Almighty, I hope this here gun fires. Made it myself. Carved my name right on it, Peter Bowen. (*Sound—Distant fife and drum march.*) . . . They're comin'! I can hear the fifes ravin'. Them drums are flailin' commands! . . . I can see their bayonets now . . . They're comin' through the long grass, up and over the first fence. That's a solid red line! Looks like they're goin' to swallow us up. Lord Almighty, when's Colonel Prescott goin' to yell fire? I can see their faces. "Oh, Lord, I thank thee for sparin' me to fight this day. Blessed be the name of the Lord"—Oh, please Lord, don't let me run!

COL. PRESCOTT. F I R E !

(*Drum roll.*)

PETER BOWEN. Fire! . . . I got one, Lord Almighty! There's a whole wall of them. I'm scared of them bayonets! Where's Issac Baldwin? This smoke's blindin' me . . . (*Guitar—under* PETER BOWEN; *tune,* Liberty Song, *slow tempo.*) got to get up to the fence . . . That Redcoat's breeches are all bloody spots. He's turnin' the little white flowers red . . . Got dirt in my mouth . . . I hurt . . . don't want to look . . . Got two more rounds.

SINGER. (*Guitar accompaniment. Tune*—Liberty Song.)
All ages shall speak with amaze and applause
Of the courage we show in support of our laws
To die we can bear but to serve we distain
For shame is to Freedom more dreadful than pain

(*Guitar—continue under* PETER BOWEN, *out at* "I hurt.")

PETER BOWEN. Got no more shots to fire. Could load it

with stones. Could try. They got bayonets. Boots. Never saw boots like that. Never had a pair of boots. Can't lift up my head. Lordy, I hurt . . . Hope my mother knows . . . hope somebody knows . . .

(*Guitar—drum rolls,* Death March *under* VOICES.)

VOICES. (*Alternate.*)
Peter Bowen
Issac Baldwin
Asa Pollard
Lucas Green

SINGER. (*Guitar accompaniment. Tune*—Johnny Has Gone For A Soldier.)
O Johnny dear has gone away,
He has gone afar across the bay,
O my heart is sad and weary today,
Johnny has gone for a soldier.

Shule, shule, shule, shule agrah,
Time can only heal my woe,
Since the lad of my heart from me did go,
O Johnny has gone for a soldier

I'll dye my dress, I'll dye it red,
And through the streets I'll beg my bread,
And through the streets I'll beg my bread,
Johnny has gone for a soldier.

Shule, shule, shule, shule agrah,
Time can only heal my woe,
Since the lad of my heart from me did go,
O Johnny has gone for a soldier.

LEMUEL GENT. They was a'scared. Them scarlet popinjays! They was a'scared of us. Prancin' down the Pomfet Road in their lobster coats with shiney buttons. They made good targets! We shot at 'em'! From behind our barns and out our windows. Widdow Weeks sneaked around the out-house, bopped a Lobster-coat with her frying pan whilst his pants was down . . . he was so surprised, he up and died right there! . . . Musket-ball wizzed right between her legs. She didn't stop. Said she was too old to tickle. Got Zeek's old musket and loaded it with stones. Said she'd get the devils who burned her church . . . ended up they burned her house too . . . Set fire to Samuel's barn . . . We lost Ike, Jude, Mary, Ruth, Ioulis . . . But we saw those Lobsters run . . . I'll never forget that . . .

SINGER. (*Guitar accompaniment. Tune,* What A Court Hath Old England.)
Then Freedom's the word, both at home and abroad,
So out every scabbard that hides a good sword.
Our forefathers gave us this freedom in hand.
And we'll die in defense of the rights of this land.
Derry down, down, down, Derry down.

(*Guitar—Continue under* Mother Lowell.)

MOTHER LOWELL. . . . Oh my, I'm afraid to turn that bend. On t'other side will be my little house . . . My knees are shakin' . . . They was right; I shouldn't have come here alone. Can't seem to put one foot in front of t'other . . . Now, it will be all right, now . . . They can't of burnt all of Charlestown.* There must be somethin' left . . . Oh, can't seem to catch my breath . . . Better sit down a minute . . . Lived in that little house for 45 years. My Emma, Seth, John all born there. Grew up there. Brought their dear children back there to play . . . Oh! . . . sounds like someone's comin'. Ridin' past my house! My Aaron? No, . . . no now, he's dead. Gone long before the British came and burned . . . There'll be somethin' of Aaron's there . . . Got to get up . . . got to go and see for myself.

(*Guitar—out.*)

* District of Boston.

JONAS COFFIN. Mother Lowell! I nearly ran you down. What you doin' back here?

MOTHER LOWELL. . . . Oh Lord, Lord . . . They was right . . . all gone . . . just the chimney and the stone step . . . oh Lord, Lord.

JONAS COFFIN. Come, Mother Lowell, there's nothin' here. Let me put you on this horse; take you back to Cambridge.

MOTHER LOWELL. . . . Got to look through . . . there'll be somethin'. The good Lord would have seen to it somethin's left . . . You just leave me alone, Jonas Coffin, and let me look . . . There, there now, there's Emma's little toy chest. Made of tin, didn't burn . . . oh . . . oh, can't open it. Fire's burned the top down shut . . . Must find our bible. Got a silver cover on it. Wouldn't of burned. Got all our families' births in it . . . I want it . . . I want my house, Jonas Coffin, I want my home back!

JONAS COFFIN. Mother Lowell, come away. This ain't no good. You'll make yourself sick again.

MOTHER LOWELL. Now you just wait a minute . . . I'll get hold of myself . . . just a minute . . . there now . . . You help me pull this out here. That's the sword Grandfather Angus brought from Scotland. I want that. I'll give it to Seth. He'll have it when he goes off with General Washington and the Continental Army. He'll have somethin' of Aaron's and of me and of this house . . . Now you go on now about your business, Jonas Coffin . . . I'll just sit here a spell. I'll be all right . . . This here was my home. I don't want to leave it just now . . . You can open this chest of Emma's for me. I want to hold her little doll . . . Aaron made that doll. You take that sword back to Seth and the Continental Army. I want that to go with George Washington and the army of free men . . . I'll just sit here a spell . . .

(*Wind—establish and continue under* VOICES.)

VOICES. (*Alternate.*)
Wallace Grey
Anthony Wolf
Luther Japhet
Julius Black
Mathias Rush
Giles Nott (*Wind—out.*)
Jeremiah Gunnon
John Beatty
Robert Love
Eleazer Crain

SINGER. (*Overlap* VOICES *at* Giles Nott. *Guitar accompaniment. Lyrics*—Granfield. *Tune—original.*)

To the Continental Army,
came peaceful men and boys.
With ears that tracked the wild deer,
they heard the cannon's noise.
But to live and breathe in freedom,
the battle must be joined.
They drove from out of Boston,
Lord Howe and John Burgoyne.

Now the Redcoats thought to split us,
the north right from the south,
And the finest place to do it
was at Great Hudson's mouth.
But our General was not napping,
and our ranks began to grow,
He moved them to Manhattan,
for a strong and forceful show.

The British brought their war ships
to float off Gravesend Bay.
Their tall masts were a forest
that dimmed the light of day.
The blazing sun of August
brought fullness to tall wheat,

But this bounteous crop of harvest
our men were not to eat.

Their blood mixed with the tall grass;
the sheaves were left unbound,
We lost . . .

RUNNER. (*Overlap on* "We Lost.")
Retreat! Retreat!
We have lost Long Island!
Miles, Sullivan, Wyllys' men flee to Brooklyn Heights
Retreat!
The line is broken
Retreat!
There is safety across the River in Manhattan
To the River!
They pour through Jamaica Pass
Retreat!
To the Boats!
To the River!
Retreat!
They come across Gowanus Swamp!
To the River
To the River

MEN. (*In darkness at* Brooklyn Landing.)
Cast off!
The current pulls
Cast off!
No more for God's sake! No more men on this boat!
We've but 3 inches of free board
Push him back, push him back now!
The man's wounded, for God's sake!
Boat full!
Break his hands! Cast off!
For God's sake, we'll be back. We've 5,000 yet to get to Manhattan!
Cast off!
Pull away, pull away

Break your backs men.
Pull for Manhattan, we've an army to move.
Pull away
Pull away

(*Sound—water, rowing, etc.*)

. . . .
. . . .
. . . .
. . . .
. . . .
. . . .
. . . .
. . . .
. . . .

MEN. (*In darkness in East River.*) . . . the cutters will see us . . . it's black . . . it's black, thank God . . . they carry light cannon . . . Hard to lee . . . Pull to lee . . . 5,000 yet to be ferried over . . . Put your backs to it men! . . . the oars are bloody, my hand slips . . . Pull to lee . . . it's a mile to Manhattan . . . how many hours til day break? . . . the tides turning to the wind . . . the sails will not make it, there'll be drownings . . . Oh God, there's a great splashing out there! Give way men! Give Way! Look Along Your Oars! Silence, Silence . . . I hear oars dip . . . No, it's a cutter! . . . get the guns . . . find the guns . . . God the powders wet . . . we're turning! We're turning! . . . We're caught in the current! . . . Pull away men . . . Pull away

(*Sound—water, rowing, etc.*)

. . . .
. . . .
. . . .
. . . .
. . . .

MEN. (*With lanterns at* South Street Landing.)
Down here! Down here!
There's 3 boats come in down here.
Bring a lantern
Bring the hooks
Pull her in

Tie her fast
More men on the hooks
Swing a light, swing a light
There's a boat missed the slip
Swing a light
Guide her in

JONATHAN STOVER. Is they men from John Haslets in that boat?

CONTINENTAL. Gives us a hand with the hooks.

JONATHAN STOVER. Be they Delewares in that boat?!

CONTINENTAL. Pull her close! Tie her fast!

JONATHAN STOVER. They Wear Red And Blue With High Cap Plates!

CONTINENTAL. No uniforms on this boat.

JONATHAN STOVER. Where's My Son? They Told Me He Be Safe!!

CONTINENTAL. Haslets men come over two hours back.

JONATHAN STOVER. No! No! Where's My Son? They told me he be safe! The enemy got all round us . . . but I held for my son . . . His name is John Stover. He Wear Haslets Red And Blue With High Cap Plates!

CONTINENTAL. We got no names. We move an army before day break. More men on the hooks.

JONATHAN STOVER. They Told Me . . . Haslets Men Be Safe If We Held At The Creek! I HELD FAST! . . . I HELD FOR MY BOY.

CONTINENTAL. Haslets men already come over. Throw a hook there, hold it fast.

JONATHAN STOVER. WHERE'S MY BOY . . . I

stayed with Mordicai Gist. Stirling fought like a wolf. I held fast for my boy! . . . Five Times They Attacked! . . . FIVE TIMES WE DROVE THEM BACK! . . . You! Boatman! My boy is with HASLET! Comes he in on your boat!?

BOATMAN #1. Smallwood's men on my boat! Try back at the stairs.

JONATHAN STOVER. He's not back at the stairs!! . . . they be marshes . . . little ponds . . . Lukus Townsend is missing . . . I can't tell if he be killed or taken or drowned . . . men sunk to their chests! MY BOY WEAR BLUE WITH HIGH CAP PLATES!! My gun wouldn't fire! Gun powder wet . . . they hunted us on horseback . . . like animals on horseback! . . . Willie Varnem stuck like a pig to a tree . . . he screamed til he died. My Gun Wouldn't Fire! Musket butt against bayonet. We Held For Haslets Men! HIS NAME IS JOHN STOVER! HE WEAR HASLET'S BLUE WITH HIGH CAP PLATES. HE'S NOT AT THE STAIRS! HE HASN'T COME OVER!

BOATMAN #2. Get more ropes! We launch again!

JONATHAN STOVER. Be They More Delwares To Come Over? They must be more Delewares!

BOATMAN #2. Haslet's men come 2 hours Back!

JONATHAN STOVER. I Asked Them! I asked them . . . swamp muck turns the jackets . . . the fall of the tide will bring up bodies . . . the tides going out. He has A Shiney High Cap Plate . . . HE BE YET TO COME OVER!! I'll help pull in here at the slip!

OFFICER. There's no more Delewares to come! We told you of your son two hours back! You're wet and you're bleeding! Get on back to the stairs!

JONATHAN STOVER. . . . my fire-piece was wet . . . Musket butt against bayonet . . . Willie Varnem stuck like a pig to a tree . . . they got all round us. Hessians come through the pass! They Told Me He Be Safe! I held fast! They Told Me Hold Fast My Boy Would Get Out!! . . . water up to my arm pits . . . our muskets wouldn't fire . . . fire-piece wet . . . His Name Is John Stover! OH GOD, HE BE YET TO COME OVER!!

OFFICER. Get this man back to the stairs! We told him his son is dead. Stirling was captured! We told you your son is dead!

JONATHAN STOVER. . . . I'll swing a light at the slip . . . I'll guide the boats in . . . they told me Haslet's men be safe if we held at the creek . . . Oh God They Come Through The Pass! . . . Miles . . . Wyll's men run . . . I held fast . . . I held fast for my boy . . . I'll swing a light . . . for the next launch . . . I'll guide my boy in . . .

(*Guitar—drum rolls under* VOICES.)

VOICES. (*Alternate*.)
John Stover
Lukus Townsend
William Varnum
Elisha Benton
Seth Rider
Ishmael Moffit
Abner Belding
Jabez Avery
Issac Potter
Degory Sparks
Charles Stump
Hosea Rigg

MAN. (*Over names and drum rolls*.)
I hate the drum's discordant sound,
Parading round, and round, and round:
To me it talks of ravaged plains,
And burning towns, and ruined swains,
And mangled limbs, and dying groans,
And widows' tears, and orphans moans;
And all that Misery's hand bestows
To fill the catalogue of human woes*

SINGER. (*Hum on open sound. Chorus of* Johnny Has Gone For A Soldier.)

*John Scott, circa 1776

. . . .
. . . .
. . . .

SINGER. (*Guitar accompaniment. Verse:* Johnny Has Gone For A Soldier.)
O here I wait on Buttermilk Hill,
And who can blame me, cry my fill
And every tear would turn a mill
Since Johnny has gone for a soldier.

(*Guitar—continue chorus of* Johnny *under* Hannah Styles.)

HANNAH STYLES. The ground is warm, warmer than the air. Full, and ready for harvesting. It's warmth stirs me. I rub my swollen belly gainst the smooth rail fence. Your strong hands smoothed the boards . . . for a moment my blood beats harder, harder . . . I slip down onto the warm moist ground. Your child moves under my heart . . . still protected and warm. Lord, let him stay safe inside me. . . . Our babies cry. Hunger stabs at their tender bodies. They starve while the crops rot for harvesting . . . I must have you home . . . God forgive me . . . I shall send Ethan 100 miles to fetch you . . . His soft hair doesn't yet brush the top of this fence . . . God forgive me. (HANNAH *retains stage focus throughout next 3 paragraphs.*)

SINGER. (*Guitar accompaniment. Verse.*)
I'll dye my dress, I'll dye it red,
And through the street I'll beg our bread
And through the street I'll beg our bread
For Johnny has gone for a soldier.

(*Guitar—out.*)

FARMER MILES. David! Bring a shovel and a pick! The ground is hard and we have burying to do! There's a little body by the side of the Albany Post Road. Just a boy, looks like. Must be he was run down by one of . . . Burgoyne's Riders . . . wonder what he was doin' out on that road? . . . so late at night . . . all alone . . . looks like . . .

SINGER. (*Guitar accompaniment. Verse.*)
Dear Lord you know I loved him so
That it broke my heart to see him go
And only time will heal my woe,
My Johnny has gone for a soldier.

MOSE PILLSBURY. (*Trying to make his piece of ground comfortable.*) It's for God damn surely we're goin to small gun-powder tomorrow! I seen the Britishers camp-fires across the gully . . . I got to get me some sleep . . . Stretch out before the hoar frost covers this here piece of ground . . . Jude Baily, Josh Driscoll don't want me to sleep near the fire. Says I smell. "Hell," I told Jude Baily, "Hell, everythin' that's alive smells. My smell keeps off the vermin" . . . God damn . . . Capt. Dole give me this piece of meat. Hell, I ain't goin' to eat it. This is Indian meat! I seen them God damn burn it on a stick. Them's Indian ways! Hell, I ain't no Indian . . . I'll eat porcupine boiled. T'ain't bad. Catch him in a bucket. Don't shoot him! Tastes queerly if you shoot him. Pull out his quills, skin him and boil him good. T'ain't half bad. Hell I'll eat a skunk if they boils it with a carrot—but I ain't no Indian. I got my ways, and this here's Indian meat! . . . We'll sniff gunpowder tomorrow, that's for sure . . . I ain't scared . . . I'm hungry! . . . If I can get a pot I'll boil my shoes. They's good hide. I'll get a carrot and some onions—make a soup. Them Marylanders got cook pots. Maybe I could sneak over quiet like and grab one while they's asleep. I got to eat somethin', even if it's only garp and swaller. I'm a big man. The rumblins in my belly sound like Knox's cannon, bet those Britishers can hear it all across Captain Vvly's gully . . . sun-up they'll swam that gully, that's for sure. Hell I ain't scared! I'll get myself some sleep ifin my belly would just stop rumblin . . . I'll go sneak a cook pot off a Marylander and make some garp and swaller . . . Sun-up we'll smell gun-powder.

(*Sound—Fife and drum play* Battle of Trenton. *4 measures.*)

. . . .
. . . .
. . . .
. . . .

(*Fife and drum continue under* OFFICER.)

OFFICER. Keep moving! Keep moving Men! We take Trenton at dawn. Stay together. Stay with your officers.

SINGER. (*Tune* Battle of Trenton.)

On Christmas day in 76
Our ragged troops with bayonets fixed
For Trenton marched away
For Trenton marched away

(*Fife and drum solo, then fade. Sound—wintry wind, establish and continue under* Morris Bent.)

MORRIS BENT. I can't see the back of Zeke Hassard's head no more . . . Just can't keep my eyes full open gainst this sleet . . . Oh God let me keep up! . . . I ain't never been so cold in my life . . . can't stop shakin' . . . Wish I hadn't torn that piece off my jacket to wrap round my feet . . . They're still oozin blood . . . Dear Christ, what I wouldn't give for shoes! A wolf could track me by my blood on the snow . . . Only Dave Timmins got a pair of real shoes . . . Wonder where he got em? He's got whole breeches too . . . got them off a Britisher.

They've got blankets . . . can't stop shakin' . . . Bet his legs don't ache . . . like mine . . . right up to my God damn belly . . . Keep goin! . . . got to keep up . . . Wait a minute, what's the countersign? . . . What're the words! . . . Can't think . . . 'Victory or Death,' that it! . . . got to remember in case I get separated . . . 'victory or death'

OFFICER. Stay together men! Stay together! No stragglers!

MORRIS BENT. Christ Almighty, that officer's got his gun on the ready—stragglers are goin' to be shot! . . . Oh God, let me keep goin! Zeke says those Hessians in Trenton will be drunk as lords from their Christmas feast . . . a feast, by God! . . . dear Jesus, can't remember when my belly's been full . . . if they's any food left on their plates, I'll eat it! . . . Damn it, I'll eat it, even if I get shot for it . . . Hope they's all drunk as lords and we can take them easy. They's lots of them, that's for sure, and we a band of scarecrows . . . Yes sir, if I sees any bread, I'm goin' to eat it . . . even if it's a crust and there's blood on it . . . I'll eat it . . . Even if I get shot for it . . . I'll eat it.

CAPT. WELLS. Men wrap something around your musket pans. The sleet's coating the muskets. If the pan's wet, the muskets won't fire!

MORRIS BENT. . . . I ain't got nothin to wrap it with . . .

CAPT. WELLS. Rip a foot of cloth off your shirts, men, and wrap your muskets!

MORRIS BENT. Christ Almighty Captain, I ain't got no shirt!

CAPT. WELLS. For God's sake, Bent, take the rags off your feet if they're dry enough! I can't send men against VonRall's garrison with muskets that won't fire! Look to your musket!

MORRIS BENT. Yes Sir, Captain Wells . . . Oh Christ

Almighty there ain't one rag on me that's dry, them ones on my feet are all bloody. I can't tear no more off my jacket . . . God knows this musket ain't goin' to spark . . . the primins a gummy paste . . . How're my goin' to get it dry? . . . I ain't and that's all there is to it . . . Hell, I won't say nothin . . . I ain't goin to be left behind. I'll swing it like a club if need be . . . Zeke Hassard, he's got a bayonet . . . I'll go by him . . . Hell, I'll swing this musket like a club and yell like a Indian . . . and if it breaks, I'll break a few Hessian heads first . . . Yes sir, I'll yell like an Indian . . . God, I wish I could get warm . . . just for a minute . . .

CAPT. WELLS. (*In distance.*) Close ranks, men! Close ranks! Fix bayonets—pass the word!

MORRIS BENT. Oh God, we're goin' to charge! . . . Lord Jesus . . . Can't get my hands to move!

CAPT. OAKS. (*In distance.*) Drummer, beat to arms! Beat for fast trot!

(*Sound—drum.*)

MORRIS BENT. Where's Zeke Hassard? Oh God, I'm not keeping up . . . There go Knox's cannon. It's begun now . . . blood's poundin' in my head . . . doesn't seem like I'm movin' . . . can't feel my legs . . . Where's Zeke Hassard? . . .

(*Sound—gunfire, etc.*)

HESSIAN. (*In distance.*)

Der Feind!	Heraus!	Heraus!
(*The enemy.*)	(*Turn out.*)	(*Turn out.*)

MORRIS BENT. They've begun! . . . They've begun! . . . the attack's begun! Without me! . . . Oh God . . . Dear Jesus, everything seems so far away . . . Oh God don't let them leave me behind . . . please

God . . . Hell, I'm cryin' like a baby . . . Can't keep up . . . What's the countersign? . . . What's the countersign? . . . (*Whispered.*) What's the countersign . . .

VOICES. (*Whispered.*)
Morris Bent
Joseph Ellis
Asa Fox
Silas Bates
Samuel Buck
Seth Turner
James Watt
William Mull
Abel Hart
Caleb Herenden
Julius River
Wallace House
John Gibson
Benjamin Dole
Asa Pollard
Mathew Cummings
Jason Russell
John Eaton

CHARACTERS. (*Over* VOICES.)

RUTH.
"young Johnny holding on to my skirts"

ELI.
"we cleared this land"

PETER.
"he's turnin' the little white flowers red"

LEMUEL.
"them scarlet popinjays' "

(*Increase pace.*)

VOICES. (*Whispered.*)
Tomas Calborn
Issac Hobart
Samuel Nelson
Asa Cram
Asahel Nins
Simeon Pike
John Alexander
Peter Fisk
William Warrin
Ceasar Bason
Daniel McGrath
Chambers Corey
Issac Adams

MOTHER LOWELL.
"he'll have somethin' of Aaron's"

MOSE.
"I'll boil my shoes"

JONATHAN.
"they got all round us"

NARRATOR. (*Over* VOICES *and* CHARACTERS.)
A tide
Of voices
Flowing
And ebbing.
The past
The present.
Voices
Unremembered
But forever
A part of us.

"A TIDE OF VOICES"

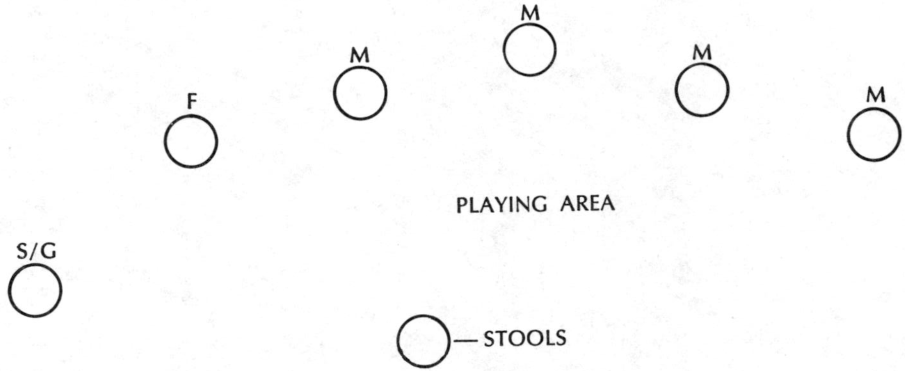

F — FEMALE
M — MALE
S/G — FEMALE SINGER/GUITARIST

All props are pantomimed.
Platforms could be used effectively to give variety to staging but are not necessary.

WHISPERINGS IN THE GRASS

"Eastward I go only by force,
but westward I go free. This
is the prevailing tendency of
my country-men. I must walk
toward Oregon."

Henry David Thoreau

CHARACTERS

HOSEA LAMB

RUTH LAMB

YOUNG MOSES LAIRD

IKE STOKES/MAN #2

JAKE MERCH

TRAIL CAPTAIN/MAN #1

MALE SINGER/Guitarist or Banjo

Whisperings In The Grass

Opening: In darkness.

Sound: Wind. Not a blowing, howling wind but an early morning rustling in the trees and in the long grass. It soon becomes possible for the audience to make out words, which sound like whispered secrets.

WHISPERING VOICES.
Great Rib
Cloud Prairie
Smoke River
Starved Rock
Glass Prairie
Buffalo Grove
Paint Creek
Hidden Gorge
Ombra Prairie
Oregon Trail
Great South Pass
Chimney Rock
Devils Gate
Roaring Gap
Silver River
Lost Mountain

(*Lights fade up on* MAN.)

MAN #1. (*Over* VOICES.) Listen . . . Listen close . . . The grass is whispering its secrets . . . Longings . . . rustling in the wind . . . Promises . . . drawing . . . drawing . . . across unpathed distance . . . to free unfenced space . . . For it is now that the eastern sparrow . . . dreams on the rustling wind . . . and like the eagle will die . . . far . . . far from the nest

SINGER. (*Tune*—Johnny Grey. *Lyrics*—Granfield.)
Blow you winds of promise
Blow you winds, blow free
In the waving grass of the prairie
The un-born wait for me

HOSEA LAMB. I had the callin. Seems like I always knowed it, but it was hidden, like the darkness inside a acorn, waitin for a piece of light to find it. Then come that terrible year, the year without a summer. Ike Stokes' wife bawled like a baby, sittin right out there on the west ridge, whimperin like a little dog. Said the Lord had turned against them. Well, it's true I ain't never seen the like. Why there was frost in July and August! It hurt my eyes to look on it. Our good Connecticute wheat turnin death white . . . Then the Lord took Seth and Ioulis . . . it was hard . . . thought I'd choke on the salt . . . My Ruth took quiet . . . sat rockin Ioulis's doll from sun to sun . . . it was hard . . . But I would not curse the Lord. He was givin me a sign. I could feel somethin growin, at last, inside of me. I set aside a spell to work it out.

WHISPERING VOICES. (*Under dialogue.*)

Great Rib
Smoke River
Glass Prairie
Buffalo Grove
Paint Creek
Hidden Gorge
Ombra Prairie
Chimney Rock
Devils Gate
Wind Mountain
(VOICES: *Out.*)

HOSEA LAMB. (*Continues after* "Buffalo Grove.")
There's open land out there in the west . . . waitin for someone to tame and harvest it . . . I heard tell the soil is as fine and black as gunpowder . . . corn could grow to 15 feet! It's the land of milk and honey! They tell me I can get three hundred and forty acres for the fourteen dollar filin fee.

Hell, I got two near grown boys and a little one. It's right for us to move on. We'll put forward as new beginners—land seekers, path finders. The Lord is tellin me to put out from New England. Settle new land like my Grand-daddy before me . . . I had my sign! We are to be new beginners . . .

SINGER. (Oh Suzannah, *Lyrics*—Granfield.)
Ho for Oregon . . .

HOSEA LAMB.
land seekers!

SINGER.
I'll find me the filing fee.
HOSEA LAMB.
path finders!
SINGER.
The clover there grows 9 feet tall . . .
HOSEA LAMB.
We go for Oregon!

(*He joins* GROUP *at rear of stage pantomiming loading wagons, in silhouette.*)

SINGER.
We pull for the western sea.

(*Sound: Rustling wind. Establish, fade slowly.*)

RUTH LAMB. It's a hard thing to leave the graves of my little ones. My Seth and Ioulis are gentled here in the soil, close with their grandfolks. I like to sit by them after the chores are done. The green hills soften slowly to shadows, and I can almost hear them sleepin; seems like they have not left me. But we have to go. Our farm is sold and we have to go. There's Elijah, Jude and young Ephriam to think of. They'll be wantin land of their own someday. We have nothin to give them. We are to join the Webner/Cross wagon train at Independence. Hosea says we are to be land seekers. I don't know if I ever sought anythin, cept maybe trailin' pine to weave into midsummer crowns for Ioulis. He reads me of Smoke River, Cloud Prairie, Wind Mountain. Sounds like singin; songs to sing to my soft-sleepin babies. They say the fields in Oregon are sky blue with wild-flowers; must be beautiful. Hosea has had a sign. I'll ask him, if they be room in the wagon, I could take a parcel of books along! I could teach the little red-men children to read. Hold them in my lap. Show them books with pictures and words underneath . . . yes . . . yes . . . warmth . . . holding close to me again. Oh my, the meadow's twinklin with fire-flies . . . jewels in a crown for Ioulis. (*Whispers.*) Oh dear Lord, watch over this hill . . . and all . . . that I leave behind . . .

(*She joins* GROUP *at rear of stage pantomiming loading wagons, in silhouette.*)

SINGER. (Johnny Grey, *Lyrics*—Granfield.)
Blow you winds, blow gentle
Blow you winds, blow free.
I cross the trackless prairie
To make a home for me.

YOUNG MOSES LAIRD. (*Pantomimes checking supplies.*) Two carpet sacks, within: one pair kip boots (too large for left foot), three pair store-bought socks (with mended toe), three hickory shirts (patched left elbow), five pounds butter crackers (lid on tight), over-large india-rubber coat, Webster Speller. Yes sir, yes sir, it's all here! Woolen pants—with gold piece sewed in? Yes, yes I can feel it. Lordy, I'm ready! I'm ready!! I could walk to Oregon! Hell, it's only twenty times more than it took to get here to the starting place. But I'll ride some in the Tanners wagon. He's got a first rate spike team . . . I can help him bull-wack. (*Pantomime biz.*) Hup! Hup! Pull! Haw! Haw! I knows how! Hell, I read about it in the pamphlet . . . Hell, I'm walkin the prairie through Great South Pass to the Continental Divide! Yippeeeeee! I'll hunt buffalo and chase Indians! (*Pantomime biz.*) Yipeeeeee! The Tanners big lead ox don't scare me a bit! I'll get him so's he's a'scared of me. (*Pantomime biz.*) Hup! Hup! Bet Mr Tanner will let me shoot his rifle. (*Pantomime biz.*) I'll stand guard. Shoot off buffalo! Better put these sacks in the Tanners wagon. Don't want to be left behind. Guess Mrs Tanner'll feed me along with everyone else. They got plenty. I saw them lay in ten sides of bacon, seventy sacks of flour, eight hams and four sack of green walnuts. I am partial to walnuts! We'll be starting soon. Yippeeeee! Don't leave without me! I'm a first rate bull wacker! (*He joins* SILHOUETTE GROUP.)

TRAIL CAPTAIN. (*He shouts to* SILHOUETTE GROUP *at rear stage.*) Turn out! Turn out!

WHISPERING VOICES.
Oregon Trail
Chimney Rock
Hidden Gorge
Glass Prairie
Paint Creek
Shining Mountain
Golden River
Devils Gate
Smoke River
Great Rib
Cloud Prairie
(VOICES: *Out.*)

SILHOUETTE GROUP. (*Over* VOICES. GROUP *pantomimes moving wagons out, prodding oxen, etc.*)
Hup thar! Pull!
Haw! Haw!
Ruth, get up on the board!
Hold the leathers, Ike!
Prod the leader!
Hup! Hup!
Turn out! Turn out!
God be praised! (*Fires gun into air.*)
Hup! Pull! Pull!
Haw! Haw!

SINGER. (*Overlap at gun shot.* Ox Drivers Song, *Lyrics*—Granfield.)
And the great adventure has begun
For 2,000 miles we'll track the sun
To the promised land—
Through 5 months of hell.
Let the bull whips crack—
And the wackers yell.
Tu mi ri, tu mi ri, tu mi ri-de-o
Tu mi ri, tu mi ri, tu mi ri-de-o
Tu mi ri-de-o, tu mi ri-de-o
Tu mi ri-de-o, tu mi ri-de-o

Our wagon wheels turn up the dust.
They carve no mark in the earth's hard crust.
That we passed by here—

No one will know.
In the waving grass—
No path will show.
Tu mi ri, tu mi ri, tu mi ri-de-o
Tu mi ri, tu mi ri, tu mi ri-de-o
Tu mi ri-de-o, tu mi ri-de-o
Tu mi ri-de-o, tu mi ri-de-o

They'll be a toll for every mile
The strong, the old, and many a child.
But crack your whip—
And give a yell.
Make the leaders draw—
Cross the gates of hell.
Tu mi ri, tu mi ri, tu mi ri-de-o
Tu mi ri, tu mi ri, tu mi ri-de-o
(*Fade and retard.*)
Tu mi ri-de-o, tu mi ri-de-o
Tu mi ri-de-o, tu mi ri-de-o

TRAIL CAPTAIN. (*He addresses* GROUP, *no longer lit in silhouette.*) Listen up! Listen up! Before we begin this morning's trek, I want all of you to hear the resolves we worked out last night. Can everyone hear me now?

JAKE MERCH. Just fine.

GROUP. (*Ad lib.*) Yes, Yes, etc.

IKE STOKES. Wait a minute, let me get up front.

TRAIL CAPTAIN. Resolved: that we pledge ourselves to assist each other through all the misfortunes that may befall us on our long and dangerous journey.

IKE STOKES. That means that Jake Merch gives me a hand if my hind wheel breaks again!

TRAIL CAPTAIN. Yes, Mr. Stokes, yes, but we must make at least ten miles a day. You mustn't hold up the train with careless driving.

IKE STOKES. I ain't careless. My oxen is careless!

(GROUP—*general laughter.*)

TRAIL CAPTAIN. Resolved: except when absolutely necessary to travel, the Christian Sabbath shall be reverently observed.

RUTH LAMB. Amen, amen indeed.

JAKE MERCH. I don't like that one.

TRAIL CAPTAIN. To continue . . .

JAKE MERCH. I didn't vote on that one . . .

TRAIL CAPTAIN. Resolved: that there shall be a sufficiency of guard appointed each night regular by the Captain.

RUTH LAMB. What do we need to guard against?

YOUNG MOSES LAIRD. Indians! (*Pantomimes shooting gun.*) Pow! Pow!

JAKE MERCH. Whoop! Waugh! I'll lick 'em. I'll take their hair!

TRAIL CAPTAIN. Resolved: that in the case of a member's dying, the assemblage shall give him a decent burial.

HOSEA LAMB. The Lord knows I didn't bring my family west to do anymore grave diggin!

TRAIL CAPTAIN. We hope no-one will need burying, Mr. Lamb. But in any event we will hold to our Christian duties and that includes burying. Let us clain up now. We follow the sun to our evening rest stop.

SINGER. (Ox Drivers Song, *Lyrics*—Granfield.)

Tu mi ri, tu mi ri, tu mi ri-de-o
Tu mi ri, tu mi ri, tu mi ri-de-o
The ox pulls slow, at his pace we go
But the devil runs, and waits below.

Tu mi ri, tu mi ri, tu mi ri-de-o
Tu mi ri, tu mi ri, tu mi ri-de-o
Tu mi ri-de-o, tu mi ri-de-o
Tu mi ri-de-o, tu mi ri-de-o

(*Guitar continues under first few lines of* IKE STOKES.)

IKE STOKES. Soon as I find that there parcel of bullets, I'm goin to barrel out into the long grass with Eb Tanner and Zeke Styles. I'm anxious to ride that new horse I traded Jake Merch for. See if we can't shoot us a buffalo. We ain't seen none of them herds yet, but their droppins is all around—chips they calls 'em. Ruth Lamb and Grandma Stokes been collectin them to burn for the cook fires. Makes a terrible black smoke and smells fierce, but they ain't no trees out here! Lord Almighty, the grass is as high as a man's waist! . . . Zeke and Mr Tanner better not start out without me. Why a man goes thirteen paces off the trail and he's fallen off the edge of the earth! Grass closes behind him and no-one can find hide nor hair. We lost John Sykes good milch cow yesterday, right after we hold up to re-iron my hind wheel. She wandered off and no-one can find her. Maybe Indians got her, or maybe she's wanderin out there in the tall grass bawlin for us. Don't intend to let that happen to me. No sir, I'll stay close by Mr Tanner and Zeke like I was chained to 'em. I'll be ridin my nice new filly. Damnation where's that parcel! Zeke, Mr Tanner, wait up for Ike Stokes!

JAKE MERCH. (*Laughs.*) That lamp-black's beginin to wear off the old nag I trades to Ike Stokes for his milch cow. He's goin to see she ain't as young and chipper as she appeared. (*Laughs.*) Puttin that ginger up under her tail sure made her lively! If he runs her after buffalo she'll be pot meat by supper. He's a damn fool anyhow. Hell, I thought Yankees were supposed to be sharp traders. (*Laughs.*) They ain't nothin compared to a Kentucky ring-tailed hollerer! A hollerer can lick his weight in wild cats! Drive a sharp bargain too, if his name be Jake Merch!

SINGER.

Tu mi ri, tu mi ri, tu mi ri-de-o

Tu mi ri, tu mi ri, tu mi ri-de-o
Tu mi ri-de-o, tu mi ri-de-o
Tu mi ri-de-o, tu mi ri-de-o

YOUNG MOSES LAIRD. (*Pantomimes prodding cattle.*) Hup! Haw. Haw! Haw!! Damnation, Haw! Hell fire and Damnation, Haw!! Haw!! Dumb, rotten beasts, Haw! Haw! Oh this ain't nothin like it said in the pamplet. Haw! Haw! Haw! Haw! Hope Mr Tanner comes back soon. Why did Ike Stokes have to get lost for anyhow! He should have stayed by Mr Tanner. Now he's rode out again lookin for him. Haw! Haw! I'll volunteer for the watch tonight. Bet that'll get me out of bull-proddin tomorrow. Hup! Hup! Wonder if them Redmen is still out there . . . (Lordy, I hope Mr Tanner comes back soon). Oh, that was a fearsome sight! Ridin in whoopin and yellin whilst we was havin our noonin stop! Lucky we still had these dumb oxen chained or they would have stampeeded. Hup, there! Hup! They was near naked and covered with vermin! (Hope Mr Tanner gets back with Ike Stokes before it's dark!) Hup! Hup! Mrs Lamb give them some corn-meal. Guess they was hungry; sucked their fingers after eatin the corn-meal, without cookin it or nothin! Wonder if they's still out there, watchin us in the long grass. Hup! Hup!

HOSEA LAMB. Moses, drive them bulls hard and chain up to the wagon in front. Eb Tanner's back. He ain't found Ike Stokes. Found his horse, all give out. But he ain't found Ike. We'll corrall the wagons early and shoot off signal guns. Maybe Ike'll find his own way back. Soon as we corrall, we'll fix to hobble the horses inside the circle and post a three-man watch. I didn't like the look of them Indians and Ike Stokes ain't found. The eye of God watches over all. Pray we ain't part of a buryin party by mornin.

MOSES LAIRD. Yes Sir, Mr Lamb. Hup there! Hup! Hell, I ain't never seen a dead man. Hup there! Hup! Hope Mr Tanner comes back to help me. I can't get the hang of chainin for corral. Hup! Hup! These bulls is gettin skitterish . . . wonder if they senses somethin waitin . . . out there in the long grass . . .

SINGER. (Ashville Junction Swano Tunnel, *Lyrics*—Granfield.)

When you hear that hoot owl squallin . . .

RUTH LAMB. Hosea, don't take the watch tonight . . .

SINGER.

Somebody's dyin, honey . . .

RUTH LAMB.

Something's watching out there . . .

SINGER.

Somebody's dyin . . .

RUTH LAMB.

The men are shooting off their rifles . . .

SINGER.

And when you hear that pistol growlin . . .

RUTH LAMB.

Guess that's for Ike to find us . . .

SINGER.

A good man's goin . . .

RUTH LAMB.

Please stay with me tonight.

SINGER.

A good man's gone.

HOSEA LAMB. I can't say to Ruth . . . I can't even touch her. I must go to shoot the signal gun for my lost neighbor . . . It's death quiet out here on the plain . . . not one bird singin or flyin . . . just the wind . . . seems like it's callin a name . . . I know it ain't mine . . . but it is the owl's call . . . I know the sound . . . the owl is again callin a name . . . callin from the deep woods beside Ike's north field in Connecticute . . . it's a hard grave I'll dig in this quiet, strange ground.

SINGER. (Ashville Junction, *Lyrics*—Granfield.)
The owl's callin
A dark Blood call.

IKE STOKES. Oh don't stop firin those guns. For God's sake don't stop lookin for me . . . They's wild things watchin . . . snuffin . . . feelin through the long grass . . . Zeke, Hosea, don't leave me out here . . . my horse give out and I can't raise up on my legs . . . can't even crawl . . . my head is bashed . . . Oh Lord, the air is moanin like a wounded thing . . . or is it me . . . Christ, it's red . . . it's red I see . . . Quiet! . . . don't make a sound . . . they's wild things lis'nin' . . . Eb, Hosea . . . quick . . . find me . . . find me . . . the wild things are sniffin close . . .

SINGER. (Ashville Junction, *Lyrics*—Granfield.)
Ombra Prairie
Sky Blue Mountain
It's all gone, honey
It's all gone.

JAKE MERCH. You tell me, what's the matter with them damn fool Yankees! We got to get us a party together and hawl in that dead horse. Hell, that's food! Meat, by Gaw!

MOSES LAIRD. Mr Merch, Ike Stokes ain't found!

JAKE MERCH. Hell, I'm talkin about the horse! She's been found. That nag was mine in the first place. I claim the right to eat her. Ike Stokes makes it back, he can have some too. I ain't niggardly.

MOSES LAIRD. Ike Stokes was Mr Lamb's friend!

JAKE MERCH. Hosea Lamb can eat his bible if that's his mind. I eats meat. I ain't goin to push up the side of the high mountains chewin on the bible. I'm goin to get me back my horse. You can come too if you've a mind.

MOSES LAIRD. Oh Ike Stokes, I hope you be found.

SINGER. (Ashville Junction, *Lyrics*—Granfield.)
A good man's dead honey . . .

RUTH LAMB. (*Soft Scream.*)
Ahhhhhhhhhhhhh

HOSEA LAMB.
Turn away, Ruth. Turn away.

SINGER.
A good man's gone.

TRAIL CAPTAIN. Moses, Hosea, dig the grave narrow and deep. We drive the oxen and wagons across the site. Pray God it cheats the wolves of the rest of their bloody feast. May poor Ike lie secure. He's a long way from home . . . and we drive half a continent before we claim our land . . .

SINGER. (Ashville Junction, *Lyrics*—Granfield.)
Golden River
Shining Mountain
Our home is west, honey
Our home is west.

(*Plays chorus:* Ox Drivers Song.)

. . . .
. . . .
. . . .
. . . .

RUTH LAMB. We travel on and on and every day it's the same . . . farther and farther from everything I know. I look out behind and it seems as if we've never passed. The grass closes behind the wagon wheels and we leave no mark. I saw three graves today . . . planks of wood from a wagon-side stuck into the ground . . . others have passed by here . . . and their graves mark a trail . . . Hosea, cholera has broken out!

TRAIL CAPTAIN. Men, drive your cattle away from the pools. They be tainted with alkali. Two of Eb Tanners ox have bloated and died.

HOSEA LAMB. Tell Eb Tanner to chain up our milch cow. She's too starved to give milk, but she can pull if need be.

TRAIL CAPTAIN. That's Christian, Mr Lamb. Don't any of you folks fill your barrels til we get to the evenin rest stop.

HOSEA LAMB. My water's all gone and my children's throats are parched.

TRAIL CAPTAIN. Tell your misses to flatten a bullet and let them suck it. It will bring the saliva.

MOSES LAIRD. Captain, Josiah Weeks has fallen off his horse. I think he be stricken. We can't bring him around.

TRAIL CAPTAIN. Lay him by and rub him vigorously.

JAKE MERCH. Hell, we tried that, Captain. He don't come round.

TRAIL CAPTAIN. Then lift him into one of the wagons and apply hot irons to his feet. He must come round. We can't tarry here.

HOSEA LAMB. We have a stricken man. We must lay by.

TRAIL CAPTAIN. The cattle will stampeed if we can't drive them to water. Chain up!

RUTH LAMB. It's an unChristian thing to drive a man to his death!

TRAIL CAPTAIN. The Lord watches over all, Mrs Lamb. We can't stop for just one man. Chain up! We drive to water.

	GROUP. (*In silhouette. Pantomimes driving wagons.*)
	Hup!
SINGER. (*Over* GROUP.)	Hup, there!
Tu mi ri, tu mi ri, tu mi ri-de-o	Haw!
Tu mi ri, tu mi ri, tu mi ri-de-o	Haw!
Tu mi ri-de-o, tu mi ri-de-o	Hup!
Tu mi ri-de-o, tu mi ri-de-o	Hup!

The trail takes a toll for every mile
Your ox, your man, your wife, your child

SINGER. (Ox Drivers Song, *Lyrics*—Granfield.)
But crack your whip—
And give a yell,
Make the leaders draw—
Cross the face of hell.

Tu mi ri, tu mi ri, tu mi ri-de-o
Tu mi ri, tu mi ri, tu mi ri-de-o
Tu mi ri-de-o, tu mi ri-de-o
Tu mi ri-de-o, tu mi ri-de-o

MOSES LAIRD. Three times today I thought I saw water . . . whole lakes of it, shimmerin out there in the sun. Mr Tanner and Mr Lamb rode out . . . It warn't nothin there! I'm seein things!! Grandma Stokes says if we kill an antelope, she'll drink the blood . . . sounds savage to me . . . She says it's the same as drinkin broth . . . but it sounds savage to me. She don't ride anymore in the wagon, says it's makin her sea-sick. There she is walkin beside the oxen. Hell, she can't walk all the way to Oregon! I think she's gettin touched in the head. I guess she's too old to be so thirsty . . . The little kids is suckin stones . . . Lordy, I hope we make the Continental Devide pretty soon. They say they are two rivers there. One flows east and one flows west. I'm goin to drink my full out of both, drink 'em right up. First I'll give some to Grandma Stokes and the kids, then drink them east, west rivers right up! I'll hold it in, not piss it out for a long spell . . . walk around . . . sloshin half east, half west . . . yes sir . . . Oh Lordy, it's gettin dark . . . It's comin up my turn to sit by Josiah Weeks. I don't like sick people . . . more especially, I don't like dead people.

GROUP. (*In silhouette.* GROUP *pantomimes driving wagons.*)
Hup!
Hup, there!
Haw!
Haw!

HOSEA LAMB. Hup! Hup!

RUTH LAMB. Hosea, we must turn back! Three in the Nevins wagon were stricken today—the two boys and the out-rider. When we do find water it's too brackish for even the oxen to drink. We lighten our load and still the bulls pull but eight miles a day! Soon it will be less.

HOSEA LAMB. Now, at noon Mr Tanner's Indian draw us a map. It shows we come to abundant water soon. I'm fixin to lighten our load again, and we will walk beside our bulls. I'll carry Ephriam.

RUTH LAMB. For Lord's sake, that was no proper map. That was a savage drawing with a stick on the ground!

HOSEA LAMB. His way, Ruth. His way. He knows the trail of the wolf and the secret cliff-nest of the eagle. He shows us where the rivers and the mountain passes be.

RUTH LAMB. Drawing like a child on the ground! . . . Hosea, the out-rider says if we don't push through Great South Pass in two days, we'll be hitting snow in the mountains. How in the Lord's name do we get our heavy Connestoga up the side of a mountain if our oxen can't get a foot hold in the snow!

HOSEA LAMB. Trust in the Lord, Ruth. He and good stout bull-rope will pull us up.

RUTH LAMB. He has seen fit to take our good neighbor and three young boys. There is sickness in every wagon. We must turn back!

HOSEA LAMB. No! . . . Ruth . . . think now . . .

RUTH LAMB. We should turn back!

HOSEA LAMB. There's more sickness behind with the tainted water!

RUTH LAMB. May the Lord and you forgive me . . . I want to go home.

HOSEA LAMB. Ruth, Ruth . . . I had a sign. Ruth, the Lord give me a sign! . . . You read the pamplet Mr Tanner's got. It says the soil in Oregon is so good you could broad cast your seed; wouldn't have to furrow it. Imagine that! The land of milk and honey waits out there! We can't turn back now . . . Oh Lord, Ruth, listen to me . . . I'm askin you. For five years I dug more rocks than potatoes out our north field. The land's wore out! Ruth, you got to believe in me. I'm askin you . . . I'm beggin you. I'm a provider. I got a strong back. I can plow from sun to sun, with no mule if need be; but I got to have land to provide. Dear God, Ruth, there's a curse on a man who buries his children! I told the Lord . . . Ruth, I'll cut off my legs 'fore I dig another hole for a baby cause I can't grow food enough to feed her! Please, Ruth, I got my chance now . . . three hundred and twenty acres of good untouched land for the fourteen dollar filin fee . . . In the Lord's name, Ruth, don't ask me to turn back . . .

SINGER. (Ashville Junction, *Lyrics*—Granfield.)
Golden River
Sky Blue Mountain
The star runs west, honey
The star runs west.

JAKE MERCH. Damnation, that Hosea Lamb is gettin on my nerves—givin me the "red-ass." "Mealy-mouths," that's what I calls them bible-toters. Damn-Yankee, mealy-mouthed, bible-toters! Now he's fixin to ask that we shares all our flour and corn-meal. No siree! Gol damn! What's mine is mine! If he fixes to share—all rightee . . . then what's his is mine—but what's mine ain't his! Waugh. Shit! It for gol-damn ain't the sick 'uns! Hell, they ain't goin to last anyhow. Figure we'll lay by one or two to cool tonight. Better to parcel out what they got then waste food on 'em . . . that Josiah Weeks now, he's got plenty of good bull rope . . . I can for sure use that. I'll just go right over and get it 'fore someone else do. Yes siree . . . Damn-Yankee, mealy-mouths . . .

SINGER. (Ox Drivers Song, *Lyrics*—Granfield.)
Crack your whip and bring the blood
The oxen slip in the rocks and mud.
Make the bulls' backs bleed—

We've a way to go,
Cross two mountain tops—
'Fore the ice and snow.

Tu mi ri, tu mi ri, tu mi ri-de-o
Tu mi ri, tu mi ri, tu mi ri-de-o
Tu mi ri-de-o, tu mi ri-de-o
Tu mi ri-de-o, tu mi ri-de-o

TRAIL CAPTAIN. Moses, unyoke the Tanner's lead ox. He's starved out, he ain't going to rise. Mr Tanner said it's all right for you to go ahead and shoot him. We'll all have a bit of meat. I can see his ribs sticking right through his skin. You can shoot a musket can't you? You won't have to aim sharp. Just put the barrel right up against his eye. Bullets are scarce. You use only one. Put the barrel against his eye. I'll get you Abe Finner's musket. (*He leaves*.)

MOSES LAIRD. No, no now wait a minute! He'll rise. I know he'll rise. (*Calling after* CAPTAIN.) I don't want Abe Finner's old musket! . . . Dumb old thing, get up! Hup! Hup! You know I mean business! Hup! Hup! Don't just look at me. Hell, I bull-wacked you all the way cross the prairie and up the bald face of the Continental Devide. Don't let your heart break now! Come on! Hell, you're the smartest of the lot. I can't do without you. Dumb old thing, you ain't drunk out of the east/west rivers yet . . . Hell! What are my doin?! It ain't Christian to talk to a beast. Get up! Hup! Hup! Hell, I got to finish with some of what we started out with. I'm losin too much . . . Mrs Tanner left that barrel of green walnuts back on the trail . . . I near bawled . . . didn't bawl when we left Ike Stokes or Josiah Weeks . . . but bawled over a barrel of walnuts . . . that ain't Christian . . . but I can't help it . . . I'm hungry . . . You now, dumb old thing, get up! Hup! Hup! I ain't goin to have supper of you. Hell, I walked side of you too long. You lost your spirit. Well . . . you'll have to get it back (*Pulls harmonica from pocket*.) and quick before the

Captain comes with Abe Finner's musket. (*Starts to play* Turkey In The Straw.) . . . Anybody come along, they goin to think I've gone feeble-minded . . . Oh well (*Continues playing chorus of* Turkey In The Straw.) . . . Oh Hell, you're starved half dead, ain't you . . . and I'm starved a mad-man, squattin here playin to you (*Plays a few more bars of* Turkey In The Straw.) . . . Oh Hell . . . all right . . . I'll shoot you if I has to. I'll get to the territory no matter what I has to shoot or eat . . . We can drag our goods in a wheel barrow like they say the Mormons do . . . It would be a hell of a lot easier if you would just get up . . . come on now . . . (*Play chorus of* Turkey In The Straw.)

. . . .

. . . .

. . . .

SINGER. (*Verse:* Turkey In The Straw, *Lyrics—* Granfield.)
Snow in the mountain,
Ice in the draw,
I et my old nag—
It near broke my jaw.
The trail is reachin up,
And I got to go—
Stake out my claim
In five feet of snow.
(*Plays chorus.*)

. . . .

. . . .

. . . .

. . . .

TRAIL CAPTAIN. Mr Lamb . . . Mr Merch . . . Moses . . . listen careful . . . there are decisions to be made. The Tanners, the Boyds, and the Nevins with their out-riders are turning back.

RUTH LAMB. Turning back! Hosea . . .

HOSEA LAMB. Wait Ruth! Captain, it's a wrong . . .

TRAIL CAPTAIN. There is no shame in turning back, Mr Lamb. It may be an act of prudence. Three trains turned back at this point last month and they had more men and wagons.

MOSES LAIRD. Then they were cowards! We ain't gonna . . .

HOSEA LAMB. Dear God, Captain, how can we turn back? We'll never make it. We got broken axles, sprayed hoops and less than half our teams! By now even the grass back on the great plains will be turned brown.

TRAIL CAPTAIN. You'll have to winter at Fort Bridger and wait for the spring grass to make the drive back to Independence.

JAKE MERCH. To what-the-hell? To what-the-hell in Independence? Waugh!! I was goin to have land of my own out in Oregon! I ain't goin back to nothin. Waugh!! I ain't goin to have it on my tombstone: Jake Merch, owner of nothin!! A man's got to own somethin! . . . some bit of land somewhere that's really his. Ask the bible toter here. (*To* HOSEA.) You tell em! . . . The first man got his ass kicked out of paradise 'cause he didn't own the land! That's the "why" there! Waugh! If you own the land nobody can throw you out—no matter what you want to eat! They's free land out there in Oregon and some of it's goin to be mine!

MOSES LAIRD. Me too! I ain't turnin back. I ain't never turnin back! They's cowards . . .

TRAIL CAPTAIN. Hold there. Think on this soberly . . . The scout tell me the snow come early in the highmost spots. We're not as far along as I calculated. If we do press on to the territory, it will be too late to plant. It will be a starving winter on our new land.

MOSES LAIRD. It ain't "our land" if we don't get out there to lay claim!

JAKE MERCH. Waugh!!

TRAIL CAPTAIN. I'm telling you that if you continue, you may well not live to stake a claim!

MOSES LAIRD. How do you know that!

TRAIL CAPTAIN. I ain't telling you what I know. I'm telling you what I think.

JAKE MERCH. There's too much thinkin goin on here! I'm gettin . . .

RUTH LAMB. If we decide to continue, will you continue with us Captain?

TRAIL CAPTAIN. No, Mrs Lamb, I'm turnin back.

RUTH LAMB. Then, Hosea, we must turn back! We have no-one to lead us.

MOSES LAIRD. We could elect a new Trail Captain! Mr Tanner's Indian drawed a map for Mr Lamb.

JAKE MERCH. A damn-Yankee, mealy-mouthed, bible-toter for a leader! Waugh! (*Spits.*)

HOSEA LAMB. There's cut-off the Indian showed me straight through Hidden Gorge to the river. If we go through instead of 'round we could figure to cut off a week.

TRAIL CAPTAIN. Mr Lamb, most likely the gorge is full of snow and impassable!

HOSEA LAMB. I'll go ahead and have a look. If it's passable we can take the wagons through and that will be our way.

MOSES LAIRD. I'll go too!

HOSEA LAMB. No need for two to go. You stay here with Mr Merch and guard the oxen and wagons. I'll leave you my rifle.

RUTH LAMB. This is a terrible, fool-hardy thing.

JAKE MERCH. All right, bible toter, we'll freeze our ass here from sun to sun . . . but no longer. If you ain't back by next sun-up, I ain't goin to be Indian meat. I'll lead on by the regular way and you catch up.

HOSEA LAMB. I'll be back long before next sun-up. (*He leaves.*)

SINGER. (I Could Not Find My Baby-O, *Lyrics*—Granfield.)

I'll track the foot of the snow-white fox,
Snow-white fox,
Snow-white fox.

I'll track the trail of the snow-white fox,
The secret path to the river-o.

(Guitar repeats chorus.)

. . . .
. . . .
. . . .
. . . .

JAKE MERCH. That bible-toter's been gone too long. We should start by the regular way. I smell snow in the air.

RUTH LAMB. Snow has no smell. Please, you shouldn't try to frighten us.

MOSES LAIRD. You promised to wait from sun to sun!

JAKE MERCH. That was if it don't start to snow. I ain't goin to squat side of the wagons til the snow covers my ass waitin for the Yankee to come back and tell us it's snowin in the gorge! Waugh!!

SINGER. (I Could Not Find My Baby-O, *Lyrics*—Granfield.)

I seek the lair of the panther cub,
Panther cub,
Panther cub.
I'll find the lair of the panther cub—
He sleeps on the breast of the snow white wind.

(Guitar repeats last line.)

. . . .

HOSEA LAMB. . . . Ruth . . . Ruth . . . the air is shining . . . it hurts my eyes . . . snow in the highmost places . . . winding soft the rocks . . . I've lost my tracks . . . not a mark . . . where-on did I come . . . the rocks . . . wool soft . . . I forgot why I come . . .

(Sound: Wind.)

WHISPERING VOICES. *(Over wind.)*

Great Rib
Glass Prairie

Flaming Gorge
Wind Mountain

HOSEA LAMB. names like singing . . . like singing . . . songs to sing to our soft sleeping babies . . . Oh Ruth . . . the snow's gut deep in the gorge . . . we'll not get through . . .

(*Sound: Wind.*)

JAKE MERCH. Chain up! The snow's two inch already. We got to go through . . . too late to go round . . . Move out!!

(*Sound: Wind.* JAKE MERCH *pantomimes prodding oxen;* RUTH LAMB *walks, bent against wind;* MOSES LAIRD *pantomimes pushing cart.*)

(*Wind: out.*)

SINGER. (Ox Drivers Song, *Lyrics*—Granfield.)
Now ends one trek that was begun.
For 2,000 miles they tracked the sun,
Through the mountain pass,
To the early snow,
Where the sun was lost
And no path did show.

Tu mi ri, tu mi ri, tu mi ri-de-o
Tu mi ri, tu mi ri, tu mi ri-de-o
Tu mi ri-de-o, tu mi ri-de-o
Tu mi ri-de-o, tu mi ri-de-o

(*Guitar continues under* MAN.)

MAN #2. There's whisperins . . . out there in the grass . . . I hear . . . though the wind is quiet . . .

There's secret rivers . . . runnin silent to a shoreless sea . . . I will walk west . . . I'll follow paths wild things know . . . I will walk west . . . There's longings . . . whisperins . . . across a grass-filled sea . . . I will walk west . . .

SILHOUETTE GROUP. (GROUP *pantomimes moving wagons out, prodding oxen, etc.*)
Turn out! Turn out!
We must cross the plains while the grass is green
Turn out! Turn out!
California or bust!
Prod the leaders!
Hup! Hup!
Wack those bulls!
To Oregon!
To California!
Chain up! Chain!

(GROUP *continues pantomime in silence.*)

SINGER. (*Overlap at* "To California!")
And so once more we start again.
Graves mark the trail without a name.

SINGER. (Ox Drivers Song, *Lyrics*—Granfield.)
What draws us on—
We do not know.
Our Star tracks west—
And we must go.

Tu mi ri, tu mi ri, tu mi ri-de-o
Tu mi ri, tu mi ri, tu mi ri-de-o
Tu mi ri-de-o, tu mi ri-de-o
Tu mi ri-de-o, tu mi ri-de-o

"WHISPERINGS IN THE GRASS"

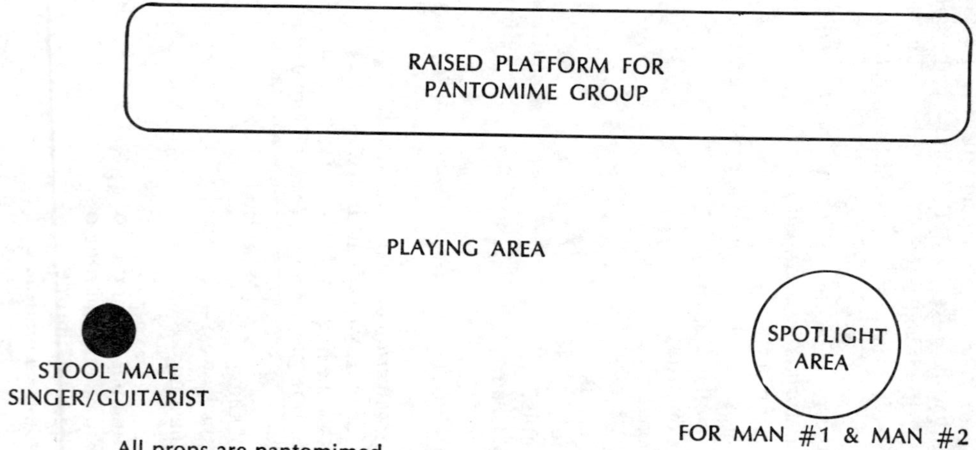

All props are pantomimed.
Figures on raised platform should be lit in silhouette.
Actors return to raised platform when not in scene being performed in playing area.
"Whispering Voices" should be on tape.

COUNT DRACULA

TED TILLER

(All Groups) Mystery comedy

7 Men, 2 Women. Interior with Small Inset

1930 Costumes (optional)

Based on Bram Stoker's 19th Century novel, "Dracula." This is a new, witty version of the classic story of a suave vampire whose passion is sinking his teeth into the throats of beautiful young women. Mina, his latest victim, is the ward of Dr. Seward in whose provincial insane asylum the terrifying action transpires. Her finance arrives from London, worried over her strange inertia and trance-like state. Equally concerned is Professor Van Helsing, specialist in rare maladies, who senses the supernatural at work. Added trouble comes from Sybil, Dr. Sewards demented, sherry-tippling sister and from Renfield, a schizophrenic inmate in league with the vampire. But how to trap this ghoul who can transform himself into a bat, materialize from fog, dissolve in mist? There are many surprising but uncomplicated stage effects, mysterious disappearances, secret panels, howling wolves, bats that fly over the audience, an unexpected murder, and magic tricks which include Dracula's vanishing in full view of the spectators.

Despite much gore, ". . . the play abounds with funny lines. There is nothing in it but entertainment."—*Springfield, Mass. News.*

ROYALTY, $50-$25

FRANKENSTEIN

TIM KELLY

(All Groups)

4 Men, 4 Women, Interior

Victor Frankenstein, a brilliant young scientist, returns to his chateau on the shores of Lake Geneva to escape some terrible pursuer. No one can shake free the dark secret that terrifies him. Not his mother, nor his financee Elizabeth, nor his best friend, Henry Clerval. Even the pleading of a gypsy girl accused of murdering Victor's younger brother falls on deaf ears, for Victor has brought into being a "Creature" made from bits and pieces of the dead! The Creature tracks Victor to his sanctuary to demand a bride to share its loneliness—one as wretched as the Creature itself. Against his better judgment, Victor agrees and soon the household is invaded by murder, despair and terror! The play opens on the wedding night of Victor and Elizabeth, the very time the Creature has sworn to kill the scientist for destroying its intended mate, and ends, weeks later, in a horrific climax of dramatic suspense! In between there is enough macabre humor to relieve the mounting tension. Perhaps the truest adaptation of Mary Shelley's classic yet. Simple to stage and a guaranteed audience pleaser.

ROYALTY, $25.00

THE SENTIMENTAL SCARECROW

(ALL GROUPS)

MUSICAL-COMEDY-FANTASY—1 ACT

Book and Lyrics by S. Charles Shertzer

and Music by Nathan Brown

A musical version of Rachel Field's "The Sentimental Scarecrow." 2 men, 5 females, and a band of gypsies. (Exterior) Modern Costumes. 5 songs, incidental music, and a gypsy dance.

The Scarecrow is exactly what the title suggests; he wishes to become a human; in order to realize his wish, he must convince some young lady to not only kiss him, but to agree to marry him. The fun of this production is found in the Scarecrow's antics as he attempts to win a wife. The music and the lyrics are delightfully amusing, plus exciting, and at times filled with genuine pathos.

The songs include "Half the Day's Gone," "A Cold Stare and a Withering Glance," "Gypsy Caravan," "I've Got to Have a Dame," and "Funny Looking."

Music on rental and deposit, write for information.
Royalty, $15-$10.

A Pink Party Dress

MUSICAL—1 ACT

David Rogers and Mark Bucci

A musical version of Margaret Bland's "Pink and Patches." 1 man, 3 females. (Exterior) Modern Costumes. 5 songs. 35 minutes.

The story of Texie, a mountain girl who hopes to escape the life of hardship and poverty her mother and other mountain women lead. She longs for the richer life she has observed at a fashionable hotel nearby and for a pink party dress instead of the patched brown denim she is forced to wear. Then a visitor to the hotel offers to give Texie a dress. Whether her proud mother will allow her to accept it and whether it will be the Pink Party Dress form the story of this charming folk musical.

The songs include "Women Folk Work Fer Men Folk," "A Pink Party Dress," "Lovely Evening, Isn't It?," and others. Complete libretto and piano score.

Royalty, $15.00 first performance
$10.00 each additional performance.

SPOON RIVER ANTHOLOGY

CHARLES AIDMAN

Conceived from EDGAR LEE MASTERS'
'Spoon River Anthology'

3 men, 2 women—A stage

Via musical interludes, we are introduced in a cemetery to the ghosts of those who were inhabitants of this town, and whose secrets have gone with them to the grave. There are 60-odd characterizations and vignettes in this constantly interesting entertainment, offering an amazingly varied array of roles and impersonations, from young lovers and preachers and teachers, to the funny chronicle of the poor mixed-up Jew who ends up in the wrong cemetery. Both the sordid and the humorous sides of life are portrayed, with fetching ballads, and the free verse form of Masters. "A dramatic presentation reduced to its simplest terms . . . moving and beautiful . . . an evening of astonishing stirring emotional satisfaction."—*N. Y. Post*. "A glowing theatre experience . . . a brooding and loving American folk poem brought to life on a stage."—*N. Y. Times*. "Vivid . . . quite an inspiration. . . . A decided novelty. . . . It has punch and humor and bitterness, and often it stabs the heart."—*N. Y. Daily News*. "Warm, radiant, poetic. . . . A compelling experience in the theatre."—*N. Y. Journal-American*. "A procession of unforgettable men and women, and a powerful evocation of life."—*N. Y. World-Telegram & Sun*.

(Royalty, $35-$25.)

DAVID *and* LISA

By JAMES REACH

Adapted from the book by THEODORE ISAAC RUBIN, and the screenplay by ELEANOR PERRY

11 men, 11 women

The production is extremely simple; it is played against drapes and uses a minimum of props. The award-winning motion picture, *David and Lisa*, has now been adapted for the stage with the utmost fidelity to its illustrious prototype. It retells, by use of the most modern stage techniques, the strange, appealing and utterly fascinating story of the two mentally-disturbed adolescents: David, only son of wealthy parents, over-protected by a dominating mother, who is tortured by his mania against being touched; and Lisa, the waif who has never known parental love, who has developed a split personality and is in effect two different girls, one of whom will speak only in childish rhymes and insists upon being spoken to in the same manner. The play follows them during the course of one term at Berkley School, where they have come under the sympathetic and understanding guidance of psychiatrist Alan Swinford and his staff; follows them through exhilarating progress and depressing retrogression; follows them—and their fellow students: Carlos, the street urchin; the over-romantic Kate; stout Sandra, and others—with laughter and heartbreak and suspense.

(Royalty, $50-$25.)